That's What Happens When You Live on Haight Street

That's What Happens When You Live on Haight Street

Antoinette Vella Payne

That's What Happens When You Live on Haight Street
⬚ 2023 Antoinette Vella Payne
ISBN: 979-8-9894172-0-9

Cover art, "Hollywood Chic"
⬚ 2003, Robert "Rosey" Rosenthal

First Edition, 2023

Printed in the United States of America

Edited by Chaeyeon Park
Cover Design by Krystle May Statler
Layout Design by Kallie Hunchman

Dedicated to Shaunna Leigh Vella,
my raison d'etre, my daughter.

Acknowledgements—

Thank you Sacred Grounds Poetry community in San Francisco. The longest running open mic in the city since 1971 offering awesome poetry every week. Many of the poems in this collection are my responses to prompts generated there.

Thank you, Hiram Sims, founder of Community Literature Initiative in Los Angeles and my cohorts in the Season Ten, National Class without whom I would not have this book to share.

Thank you, Frank and Deanne of the 1428 Haight Cafe at 1428 Haight Street, S.F. who have supported poetry at the cafe, curated by none other than me. I and others continue this reading in memory of the late Richard Sanderell who began the venue. We do a monthly hybrid reading there both in-person and on Zoom. Thank you to Dan Brady for his continued Zoom support for this venue.

These poems have been published in San Francisco's *Haight Ashbury Literary Journal* : "Maltese Migrations," "New November for an Old Soul," and "Stardust."

These poems have appeared in the online publication of *Poetry Express Newsletter*. From Survivor's Poetry in London: "Lies," "Ars Poetica," "Falling," "Story of Things," "Dream Didactic," "Digging Deep," "My Other Mother," "Underground Temples," "On Arrival," "Online Dating," "Stardust" and "Opinion."

S.L. Mc Gill, Poet and Edward Mycue, Poet—Thank you for your kind endorsement(s) on the back cover.

Thank you Rosey Rosenthal for providing the cover art.

I.

Preface—

Living in the iconic San Francisco Haight Ashbury district, these poems depict the scenes and people I see every day, as well as my thoughts on sex, love, family, friends, spirituality, consciousness, and the human experience.

As a 40 year student of *A Course in Miracles*, many of my poems reflect humanity's connections to divine consciousness and the serendipitous events that make life meaningful and interesting. In this book, I will take you through a series of poems utilizing a stream of consciousness verse and word play sharing personal stories and other reflections that will stimulate memories and insights of your own.

That's What Happens When You Live on Haight Street

I.

In Cahoots with Divine Will

I made lunch for you
In a brown paper bag—
It looks like a poem
nourishing your day

Telling of final vibrant years
Tethered in hookups
between egocentric men and
My own egoic needs—

Integrity ever whole
Missing nothing
like the moon's form
completed by parts unseen.

Joy unequivocal to spirit—
Fear and worry bring me down
Living the grand illusion that
All are separate—

Perfect silence fills a void
Bone arrow sparkling rod
Fingertip connectors misfire to
an intentional collective

Each affecting the other
Offering up light as the
dark within disperses
I take my pleasure

In gratitude I am Spirit
flickering, congealed with you
as both teacher and student
trusting in life's curriculum.

New November for an Old Soul

The leaves are bright—
Changing colors rust to red,
Letting go, leaning into
what's next

Moving on to what serves them
Now, in this new November,
Apple orchards smell sweet
Carved pumpkins sit on the porch

And like the fall leaves
            fluttering to the ground,
I am falling into myself
This November hour of my life

Looking for sustenance of spirit,
In kindness & connection
The part of me that looks like you,
Different yet the same

Reconnoitering the landscape of your body
Falling into the curve & crevice,
Of your smile, brighter than the sun
Fluid as time lapsed over eons

I literally have to look,
Into your eyes
Cool like chill November,
As you pretend not to know me

I am the second full moon
Call me blue—
Blessing you with renewal,
Pushing toward possibility

Look at me this November night,
Feel my rays on your face
Contemplate my rare return,
Take a moon bath—look up

Valentine Fine Tuned

I am God's son whom he loves[1]—
The Holy Spirit my friend
She is a golden snake
Like Osiris, sun goddess

She allows me curiosity
Sends lessons through unlikely messengers
My hands and feet at her command
My tongue her whip.

Pray I am kind
Before my oppressor
Lay down in submission
"Be polite," he says

Couch your words in sugar
Direct light will dry them out
Harden their edges
Put creases where punctuation belongs

Read between lines
As space fills a void
Forest's fallen leaves
Litter and cushion my soul

My partner, my lover
my teacher, my destiny
Connection begins with you
Microcosm of my place in line

From your Valentine shrouded in love
Revived from Lupercalia, she wolf
Celebrated in blood sacrifice
Wiped clean with milk

Saint Valentine affirms new life in procreation
Transformed to red heart-shaped box
With white snowflake designs
Filled with chocolates to give.

Stardust

Winter's darkness falls asunder
Spring brings in the light
Ishtar's ancient name resides in me
Without ignorance or ego

I am determined to see
Obeying no laws save nature and change
My eyes do not see
The Light

I am not a body^2
But what am I?
Love and light essentially joined
In spirit housed in flesh

Everything trimmed in light
Glitters away the dark
Shows what's hidden
Yet always there

Compassion's subtle shimmer
Radiates in my voice
My stance and stride
Curiosity brings worldly gifts

Melons and grapes
Sweet sizzling summers
Rites of spring
When the wind breaks

Sky wide open wide
There is nothing but
The light
You and I as co conspirators

Hold this dream to
Billow out from under our flaming
Fortuitous fraction of time
Detonated at birth we are exploding stars

my two hearts

one heart holds promise and dreams
all things rooted in future events
destiny worshiped on separation's alter
                    inside this heart

i relinquish one path so another will show
i hold myself lone without influence
i visualize streets walked, neighborhoods
                    i know and some just visited

connections that have passed
stay in this heart
cherished moments i recall
in this place where memories grow fonder

        like the duplicity of ventricles and chambers
behind this familiar heart
deep under back ribs
similar beats pound in my ears

skip one jump two i can hear it under my breath
new ventures give rise
to new wisdom
        in this second heart—

sights and sounds sense the afternoon light
falter across a green expanse
along with hard answers
how to shed my skin for the next life?

will the world survive herself?
will Self love survive the world?
all things are lessons
          in this second heart

i vibrate & glow red with romantic love—
family's affection
friends gather under one same Source
          in this second heart

Sex in the Bathtub

Naked glistening soft skin
Bubbles overflowed to your face
Scrunched and striving
I don't mind I don't mind
      In the bathtub
You do not speak
Or care for me at all
Perhaps you think I am
      Sad old woman
Without self respect
To have sex in the bathtub with a stranger
      You are wrong
      I am

          Have been
              Walk with
                  Stand in
                     Love
Sashay on excursion where
Enormous fiery stars like my orgasm
Blast
Under the sea wet and wild
Holding my place secure
In the scheme of human kindness

Pictures Lie

We met again thirty-seven years
After we hooked up
You thought I was another groupie then
Promiscuity my calling card

Don't we just love ancestry.com?
Uncovered truth through DNA
You called to say, "Hey we might've made a miracle"
Without doubt she is that

I was looking for love outside
My broken self
Today we sit arm in arm on your couch
Smile at our daughter in a photo on her iPhone

You remind me how you haven't
Changed a bit in thirty-seven years
I remind you
I wouldn't know it if you had

We are all so California accepting of grace
Attesting to this event that changed
Me forever
Made me momma

Your family and mine merged
My child created in love
By mySelf
You were just the tool

Me the 1980s unwed mom
Living in the sexual revolution
Pretty sure it was the other guy
Someone my parents knew

It didn't matter she was mine
DNA set the record straight
We do not like him as much as we like you
Thank you very much for your genes

My Baby

She came to me out of desire
Manifestation

Seeded from need
Created through intention

This child
Blue eyed blond girl

So unlike my Maltese brown
Undeniably mine

A gazelle in a family of hippopotami
Side by side we grew our wings

In flight as if she drew the map
To escape my stifled style

Decoded acceptance of every part
Of me where dreams start out

Lacking trust
Hoping that control—taking matters in

My hands age faster than my heart
Recalling God's promise

If dreams hold love as the answer
Guidance comes to provide

Each day breaks open the sky
In concert we walk

Remembering every dream
Turned blessing

Fat Girl

Fat girl wears hats of illusion
Promised burden belonging to can't
ride bikes, wear shorts
eat in front of people

No dancing either
My compulsive addictions rule
My hungry heart
smoldering fire within

Can't live, can't love
dis-affection at every turn
persecuted with prejudice
I am Fat girl

Isolated
Spiraling to my best friend
Sugar ladened deep fried
foster's freeze

Brought home to stuff crevices
caused by neglect
I wore a solitary verve without expectation
Never more do I lie

About the one who dismissed myself
Beneath the fair, the slim and beautiful
I am Fat girl
I am worthy of love

Fading Flowers

I have little bits of you
In me
Your poems

Pasted to my prayer book
Recalling
Rigid rules formed and forgotten

My eyes silver
Bullets
Soak daybreak up in blood

Washed across turning
Tides
A new day

Breaks
My heart open
Wide

I do not use
My body's eyes to see
Today

Forgiveness from the heart
Shoots through
This world of broken promises

One Million Skies Away

Last night two great horned owls flew
back & forth testing my tracking skills
Listening to their hoots in the same park
Everyday for years

I'm learning nature's cycles
a new & pure perspective
to grieve in various stages—
trees letting go their leaves,

Baby birds fly away,
One may be taken as a meal,
Cycles continue on to next season when a
fresh batch of new shows up for view

Nature can never be as harsh as
what humankind can grieve
Soaking in mineral baths,the
Smell of rotten eggs rises up to

Sorrow, devastation,death dismemberment
Modern day savagery inflicted
On innocents while a
Helpless world looks on

Another layer of evil
Crossbarred in the news
Headed straight for the Holy Land
Victims turned oppressor group

Like the great horned owl's overlook
Calling into the night, "This is war ", he says
"But is that reason enough
to side with other than life?"

Black Sergeant Major Movie

All hatred dispatched
between Confederates and Union sides
Our civil war ravaged big country
slavery and emancipation at odds.

Murderous betrayal by General
Charles Sanford Smithers, rabid racist,
denied 37 negro Confederates the same
escape route as white soldiers under attack.

Black Sergeant Major, bounty hunter, killer
Has no mercy either—delights in cruelty,
his response to Southern cracker aggressors—
To kill racist whites to avenge black deaths.

Cowboy days in big country
barrel of a shotgun in your face—
Saloons & churches dot open space
barracks made of wood...

Burned to the ground by black Sergeant Major
while 27 white prisoners & guards slept.
As serendipity would have it in the movies,
Sergeant Major met General Smithers' boy

All grownup and stupidly boasting about his daddy.
Sergeant Major laughed as he inflicted
revenge on that boy, retribution for
every black life ever taken away in slavery.

One hundred fifty years later
Juneteenth a modern-day holiday
Celebrating freedom, emancipation
A declaration of racial wrongs acknowledged—

Oppression of black and brown people
Lives on past history or what's seen in movies
Racism remains in America
Let us dismantle this paradigm now—

Juneteenth a door to mutual respect
Gateway to equality
Human to human
In our essence beneath our skin

We have everything
We give everything
We are everything
To deny this is to deny truth as true.

Concatenation

Universal foot path leads me
To acceptance
Grasp what's right and true
Size up my dream direction

Follow boon and tars
Spirited night's suspense
Holding hidden agendas
Where anything can happen

Muni's overhead light rumbles past
Street smart man convinced
I should fly away while I can
He fears timelessness

Yet we boomers excel
At doing nothing
Hanging out
Flying high

Stretched time pulled long
Without end
Stalk the North Star
Bright and brilliant

Party of poets concatenate
Paper doll trail
Linked by stories
Integrated anthologies

Illuminated
Singular unique particles
Voices enhanced by many
Fruitful in verse and song

Harbinger of Hope

Leave miracle making
To The One—
Waiting on welcome
Willing to hold space

My soulmate sea—
Cold pressed days
Settles into crevices
Blowing seed to bubble

Walking the blue green vastness
Calling out to be heard
Listening through ether for
Trusted guidance

Intention manifested—
Dissolving skin
I am spirit
Rocking ages upon ages

Cosmic spray above the light
Leaving time behind
Linear travel between
Conductors those who use

Miracles for themselves
Extended to others
Without regard to size
Large or small matters not at all

Only self-acceptance leads
To awareness of reality
Reparations requiring nothing more than
Truth as minor inducement

To throw that first stone
Saint Stephen got it right
Dispelling illusions on
How not to do life

Fear of death
A misplaced hostage for
Effervescent exhilaration telling
Ourselves superiority is a thing

I'm floating like in a dream
Further past shores edge
Cast about to pounding heart
Waves walk right through me

Houseless 2023

Older bodies
walk around carrying
their blankets and bags
Some are pushing a walker

Out in the elements
Huddled in doorways
Dumpster diving
Can we show compassion?

Cost of living continues to
Sky-rise-to where
Some just can't keep up
Humans need shelter

I know an older man and woman
Who live on Haight Street
They sit in lawn chairs
Every day with their dog at their feet

I've seen houseless folks walk by
Looking like their
Living room was not that long ago
Where they kept books and lamps

After the theater
walking to the metro
rats crawl from the sewer grate
past people spread out on the sidewalk

Giving Witness

Ordinary quiet comes
After the last breath
Silence like crescendo's end
Yesterday's clothes

Chosen at birth
Dropped at the door
Opened to expanse where
All of creation sleeps

Here blushed hues
Sweet horns smell translucence
Comforted like a relieved itch
Tiny bells glitter a path

Roaring light surrounds
Warm caverns hold worlds
Outstretched to no end
There are greeters

Today a tiny shard of glass from
Earlier crash finds
Calloused heal underfoot
Imbedded then removed like life

Jumpstart in Three Words

It's raining clitoris
Purple winter solstice
Holding space these last few days
Cherry blossomed into the next round

Finding joy in touch
Bone cracking cold
Chilled & dried ruffles our longings
Rubbing ourselves warm

            Your breath pushed up close in my mouth
            Tongues teased & hovering wanting more

We tumble over what's unknown
Leaving everything unsaid
      Staying present to this beautiful life
      The one we brought with us to this moment

      You are delightful
And you know it in your smile
      Your beautifully formed
      Stick shift, hard on pointed to heaven

Playing with Fire

I want to be your matchstick.
Striking you alert
Guarded in the latitudes
Of our minds

Where we risk feeling
Judged or rejected
I want you to light up
When I enter the room

Dazzled from the stars
Taken energetically
Tangled with invisible wire
Made of copper and sunshine

Pipe dreams laid down first
Foundations built on trust
Where growth can stem
In our conjoined heart

Spitting out wooden words in
Blue flamed corridors
Made of sulfur and powdered glass
Strike it hard—

Sparks fly flames ignite
Hot impersonations
Pretend we are artificial light
Decimated in the dark dense night

I want to be your matchstick.
Trusting you to see the
Corrugated edges of my mask
Hardened by survival

Talk of Love

At the end of the day.
Small talk in a wireless world—
"Goodbye Bill,
Goodbye Antoinette—goodbye."

Flirting to the end
—blatant brazen audacious chambers
Caution alerted, a tentative dance—
Flirting in desire

What if self-reliance is a lie?
Mended when we honor another—
Coming in from a California cold spell
A shallow rendition of denial.

I heard it when you said
You're not there.
Your kisses say otherwise—
Halt my breath make me weak to the marrow

Is that all me?
Laying belly to belly,
my interpretation an embellishment
claiming a hunch I want to be true.

I wrap you in my goodbyes,
I would say I love you
if it were not too soon—
to talk of love.

Falling

Cold dark January
Wake up smelling
Early morning drizzle

Someone burning overcast skies
Speed checked Akashic records
Tied to seasonal aromas in rural lands

Camped near Big Sur
Tarot cards by firelight
Shaping life's trajectory

Before divorce was real
Pulled the death card, benevolent–
Premeditated new beginnings

Shared in childhood recollections
Dimming memory's sincerity
Driving over the bridge

The one that fell in nineteen eighty-nine
Peering over its edge into
Society's prism

Like acacia's yellow bloom growing underwater
Intuition wells up behind your beautiful eyes
Recalling our past lives together

Story of Things

Evil Gollum in Lord of the Rings
Kept his precious gold ring on hand

Until it dropped to the watery cave
Below the sink hole captured by its glint

Trinket, lacquered enamel cut glass studded frog
Opens to green glazed gut to keep tiny treasures

Favorite adornments worn take on our smell
Slip onto fingers shaped in contour

Center diamond star hovering sun goddess
Faces the dove, she smiles

Artist's stamp on inside band, it says his name
Will Power, someone's illusionary strength

Transmigrated held for decades through
Conversation's tangible trust in elders' desire

She was hot, just his type, thirty years his junior
He walked away and regret set in,

Cradling turquoise studded pocket knife in his palm
Soothing keepsake held in avoidance of a lurking affair.

Steamy Window

Kettle water boils too long
Dimming sadness in
Marigold's faltering hues
Wilted while obscured

Windows look inward
Steamy afterthoughts of
Crusty men find solace in tea leaves
Tales of love remembered and hoped for—

Add milk and honey
Sweetness like a kiss
Finds fortuitous fragrances
Pumpkin spice in fallen leaves

Forlorn party girls salute
Never ending figurines of themselves
Marching home in cold dark spaces
Missed when sunshine was abundant

Cold Mercy

Two-dollar bag of marshmallows
Given to dreadlock man—
Took those sweet spongy blobs
Down wind slashed tent row.

I drive away looking back
Ashamed it's not more
Louis Longfellow lifts
Comfort's camouflage half mast pants

Up across Highway One
Eyes on Ocean
Beach access fosters
Impossible catalysts to survival

Sugar restarts motor like crankshaft
Smell of diesel
Soot spots lungs
One hundred dalmatians under fire

In his chest
Breath held on reserve strengthens
Resolve that any small kindness can
Reverse large mistakes

After years of living behind bars
With murderers and thieves
To know in the heart of man that
Love forgotten is just a spell

II.

Digging Deep

What I pulled out—
Was the forgiving of my mother,
Street lady
Living a block off Haight on Masonic

Suburbanite at twenty-two, I met my
Crazy street lady mom
At her halfway house.
Nothing halfway about it.

Nineteen fifties she left her
Husband and three kids
She stayed at the state hospital
And didn't get better.

Followed by forty years
Living next door to Saint Agnes,
Stringing rosary beads, drinking
Holy water she sheltered her mind.

Broken not right in the head.
They told us she was dead,
Suspecting otherwise I found her—
Forgave her for them.

She forgave them too
My dad for divorcing her
Then marrying another,
My Holocaust surviving step mother.

How to navigate compounded trauma?
Resilient codependence my legacy.
We were as fine as we could be
Swirling those crazy genes.

My Other Mother

Escaped Paris after Hitler murdered her family,
Gasping ghosts breeze
through
her hiding places in the dark years.

She could be the one that bore me
Or the one that wanted
children—
Married into our little family

We needed her as much as she did us
Forging bridges across
oceans
Sailed to San Francisco she met my dad.

Sometimes an evil stepmother,
Love always the undercurrent

Four feet-eleven, French accent
Listened to our stories
Answered children's question in *ancient*
tongues broken heirlooms she was, our
savior—

Obliterated to a thousand
puzzle pieces,
—Irrationally furious when my brother
bought a German made car
in nineteen sixty-nine

Decades later at ninety she died at our family
home
Dark like an old bloody skeleton.
Declared herself an atheist after living Nazi
atrocities

Hermit seed wanders in memories
Sweet golden demise
"Oh mon Dieu," she cried in anguish

Calling to a god she could not rely on.
Compounded trauma
Complicated relations

Sweeping air grabs winter's sunset
From a huge hill of fallen dollars.
Looking like dementia, schizophrenia,anorexia

Codependence for all.
Floating twigs
form bodies from shadows

Naked veils look enchanted
Water me some smoke embellished spirit,
Circling our ancestors, our progeny.

All Things Are Lessons

I stopped feeling
When she went away
Tiny girl left with needs unmet

My dad said, "Fuck foster care."
He kept his three kids together, hired housekeepers
to watch us while he worked, heart broken.

I learned to refuse myself
Take the back seat blinked through hot tears
Bottled up—unable to speak.

Crouched behind the sofa
Sneaking mayo sandwiches
I made for myself—

Afraid they would scold, I lay myself aside
Like a possum playing dead
Surviving.

Today I am your confidant your attendant
Neglecting myself, I eat to elude what I cannot feel
I surrender, I write.

When You're Dependent on Miracles to Survive

Miracles swirl about
Smashing needs to smithereens
Honing telepathic talents
Wanting more than survival

Exasperated ventilated complicated
Maneuvered predictions step aside for
Five hundred thousand lives taken
Pandemic's original message realized

Twenty-twenty spent
Twenty-one present for self care
Grim forecast to follow
Layers of change at hand

Blessed rain washes empty streets
Homes trimmed in white lights pretend
Our street neighbors gone off for a better life
Boxing Day wakes up on Haight

It can't be easy this winter
With nowhere to shelter in place
Be safe they say
Hide from infectious contagious

Indiscriminate foe
Long ago an old man predicted
Humans would be defeated by
Microscopic organisms carrying baseball bats

Freeze fragmented memories
Kept in your heart
Especially those we hold as separate
As we flee tsunamis' crest

True Labor

Woman labors behind closed doors
Pain floats upward
Held in a blue pitcher
Seeping like cream, thick and rich,

Every second shifts further from
Cozy nine-month security—
Breath calls him out with deep long moans,
Like sirens calling over vast seas

She sings him real,
Taking his time
Small soft infant smell
Cries separate self into being.

Ars Poetica

If poetry saves your soul
Held dear in perpetuity
She is raison d'etre
Both plan and purpose—

We live
To tell our tales
When memory fades
Presence to the page is left

How many words
Does it take to build permission?
Webster and Roget's
Walk arm in arm expressionless and alert

Looking for clues
In rhyme in cadence
Reason cuffed in meaninglessness
Fading beauty like flower's edge in tinted decay,

Poetry visions allure
Everlasting upon ages
Both tangible and ethereal
Awakened rallied aroused

Prime signs of value
Hearts fortified in song
Stepping stones to
Eternity

We are part of many
Letting words breathe us
Built in the whole ocean of life
Trusting we will find our way

Everyone letting down walls
We think keep us safe
Didn't see you coming,
I kind of like it.

Online Dating

I lost a few days
Talking to men online
Potential hyenas possible lovers
Uncaring of my state of mind

I have butterflies in the garden
White or orange with detailed tattoos
Hovering near the hedge that hides me from view
where two women walk by laughing,

"You better shape up
Cause I need a man
My mind is set on you"

Floating visions wonder here
I need a chalupa
Of Taco Bell fame
Last meal before jumping into the sea

Refreshed and wet
Coming up for air
I throw my head back
In time for a swallow

Before a slimy serpent wearing green scales
Rides me home through blocks uphill
Only to find my garden tomatoes
Need water under their canopy of hope

Some sweet some sour
Clue me into the cosmic flow
Dahlias scream in flaming color
Covering the fool's gold

Moving Feet

Like gay men and the Castro
Pictures and words go together
I was a typewriter that drew
details that smart people could catch

Liberal tolerant spiritual open-minded folks
Remembering God somehow
Without knowing why
San Francisco called me home

After thirty years I'm back, I'm happy
Inspired by a dream community I did not know
No one cares what you wear on Haight Street
Mirrored in storefront glass

Taking selfies in the rain
Obsessed with how I look
Giving all credit to image
An outsider that will age and die

Who needs a typewriter now
with keys ambivalent to color
City bound without a clue
Latching on to details I made

Blistered feet in new shoes
Blue suede high tops
Soft leather boots lined in
fleece water resistant keeping me hot

Partners in crime stretched to fit
Vowed to carry the weight
Upright
Sometimes limping is the only way home

Trusting myself
Without knowing why
I showed up on your doorstep flowers in hand
Words scribbled all over my feet

When You Live on Haight Street

Ghosts of wanna be flower children
Sit on sidewalks cushioned by dirty bedrolls,
Soiled hands take loose change
Our guilt offers only what we do not need

Ghosts of Jimmy Janice and Jerry
Watch for a pile of dollars dropped
To open cases where silver collects,
Strumming musical magic alive on hope

Proud and poor
Sit outside cafes
Holding pleading signs,
Your boxed lasagna will do

Ghosts of those who came to die,
Those among us still and who are yet to come—
Whisper to tourists shopping souvenirs
Claiming presence at Haight & Ashbury.

Fifty years later still wearing bell bottoms
Strolling the Haight where Ben& Jerry's sells
eight-dollar ice cream cones to pay the rent—
Where did those hippie dreams go?

Love power flower power—
Was it so radical then to value community
more than money?
Escalated real estate broke that dream

Down to the rich get richer
at Haight & Ashbury—
Where no one cares what you wear
Or if you have a home.

Lies

There was a time in my life
when I didn't know who I was
So I lied about it
Who was I fooling?

My fake French accent
Got me out of a ticket
Don't know how he fell for it
My lies morphed into truth

        Stories made real with
        imagined beginnings

I pretended I was not fat
Acted like I was not angry
Believed I was stupid
Knew myself as unworthy

        My projections crystallized
        Protecting my freedom I kept moving

I walked neighborhoods
Bedroll on my back
Scrounged for food in trash
Peed from behind parked cars

        Is it possible I shifted from one dream to
        another without waking?

Notwithstanding national lies
Formulated then repeated over time
They tried to dazzle us with their brilliance
Distract us with caged children

Facts rooted in authenticity
force pretense to disappear

Barring campaign promises
Looking past the obvious
Lurking conflicts peered out
From inside hard conversations

To follow my heart
Even to unknown ends
Proved my best path
Just an inkling of foresight

An inner knowing
Faith in the blessing of my life

At times prayer was my only food
To be seen my constant motivation
Truth my most strategic maneuver
Biden won in twenty-one

That's a fact

Talking Volcanoes with Hector

Ruptured crust where
Hot lava, volcanic ash, gasses move through
Obsidian chamber below surface
Underwater

Key lu ee a—ever constant ascent like
Killer whale spray
Vesuvio Roma where they grow slender tomatoes
Sandwiched for soft smelly cheese on hard bread

Kids play with snakes, alligators, ants—
Bee stings shoot right through them
At Panama's Jungle Warfare Training Center
for Survival

Decades forward Golden Gate Park bench
Two Blue Jays know his gait,
He tries to whistle to them with no teeth—
They whisper back, "Hey lizard man"

Truth is not forgetting
Who we are
Where we come from
Your Puerto Rico homecoming

Recalled like leapfrog in good ol' days
Homeward bound
Your place held dear in yearning forth
Reminiscent past and ever present

Si monumentum requiris circumspice
If it's monuments you require just look around—
Epitaph of Christopher Wren 1782—St. Paul's Cathedral.

Autumn in the City

October wind picks
Dry leaves up out and about
God's whisper blows through

Ruth(s)

Top secret
I should not even be telling you this
My authentic self
Me consistently who I am
Trusting in The One
Without judging
Because I can't
I am not overseer
With all knowledge

I sit on my street
Watching,
Calling hello to my neighbor
Who walks past on her way to the
Gold Cane
At eighty-six she enjoys her gin and tonic
Everyday walking to the bar
Sometimes she sits on her front stoop
In the afternoon sun and we talk
My other friend Ruth
Wrote a book inspired by My Life
It is going to be a Netflix movie.

Rocky

So dirty always in dark clothes
Fighting with voices
Sitting on a green bench in the park

Cushioned by the sleeping bag
I gave him last winter
Always walking or sitting—

Sometimes by the trash cans, he stands
Almost invisible like one of the trees,
Eucalyptus shade filters through

Cobalt skies over blocks of green expanse
Rocky disappears into the day
Twice Invisible.

Sunset's Wide Grin

Ocean Beach at dusk
White foam crawls cold
My bare feet hear
The End is near

Sinking sand washes back
Over toes under waves
Ocean sees the long view
She laps herself further out

Touches the hem of a rose color sky
Enhanced by fire fermentation
Setting sun at dusk
Faith and hope are challenged

I watch and wait
No bigger than a minute
Before artist brush dips
Clean from blue green

Drips red like blood
Shark senses me there
The sequel
Standing close to shore

At dusk it's hard to see
Light confesses dark too soon
Wide toothed heads my way
He does not confide in me

Reseeding Possibility

My hairdresser
Went back to school online
To be a drug counselor

In the Haight
Where need is great
Closed down by the pandemic

When he found himself
Walking with the spoken word
Masked and dangerous

Taking a plunge
Pushing aside the edges
Like a breaststroke underwater

Then rising to the top
Above ground
Oh so ready to breathe

4/20

Looking over our shoulders
Eyes on spies
Are you a narc? A boy asked
No I inhaled just quiet & awkward,

Twenty minutes past four
Schools out and we're
Under the bleachers—
See you there at 4/20, nineteen sixty-nine.

Fast forward fifty-four years
Haight street wild and woozy
Robin Williams Meadow shakes and rolls
Prevention to the wind billowing smoke

As incarcerated users are still in,
Helicopters rack rack racketeer overhead
Cannabis sales soar
Herbal remedy of body and mind

In the park—
They closed the tunnel gate
to Hippy Hill—
So you could go the long way over

Or sit on the knoll in the sun,
Listen to a symphony of sound, live in person
Vendors hawking bottled water
Moms reeling in their kids,

She's calling to Rhythm
A barefoot toddler who's
holding a branch looking at me—
Smooth blues escape the many boom boxes

Westward, Hippy Hill shouts
the concert's almost over—
Twenty thousand people and no masks
I leave now while I can

Heading home on Stanyan Street
Everyone else goes south to Haight
I walk against the grain
I see I am the other

Looking like white privilege
As I walk through the crowd
Among these brown and black faces
Walking my dog like I haven't a care–

High priced housing pushed many away
Now just five percent of the current population
living in the city is African American,
Eighty percent nonwhite minorities now majority—

Take that strength-
Use it for good in positions of influence,
These faces that came to the Haight today
From Daly City or Vallejo or somewhere else to

Celebrate the freedom to get high on 4/20.
Mayor's controls in place—
Helicopters overhead
ID's checked at the gate,

Could be riots in the street, but
we're talking
weed here—
It's all pretty mellow.

Holy Instants

I wasn't seeing the pennies on the ground
Until I reminded myself to give a thought to God
A shiny silver dime lay right there on my path—

My dog sniffed up the knoll
                There stood a young man in
long black coat, I did not walk further before begging his pardon

He called out to me,
                "Happy Saint Patrick's Day"
I told him the same and that I had no green to wear

Looking down he pointed and grinned
"You're standing on it, God's green earth—
Peace be with you sister"

I walk past two nerdy students falling in love
Stylish gender fluid—black tights, patent
leather shoes trendy bag nods at me

Flashy rocker struts her fabulous form
Asian lady laughing, waves to me
Kids soccer practice is over and we all go home but
him.

In the Air

Read down, then up, with the title in between.

Worldwide burden heavy with anguish
Unseen spirit bodies clamor
Parallels to fetus quickening
Letting her know life flutters adjacent

No matter the sequence
Grab your share
Handling your talent's profit
Where joy resides

Why hold back
Watching glittered hands create
An instant of this private passion
Feeling grounded in the unfurling

Songbirds creating space
Under wings flung wide
Pushing clouds into pictures
Imagined from below

Holding ground we're invincible
Wanderers finding presence elusive
Flirtations with ideas and memories
Clinch world events into place

Small daily tasks
Give substance to time
Blown out of proportion
Like an artist's thumbnail in retrospect

Can we see past our own identity
This face that looks like many
Yet its own never seen straight out
Myself locked inside perceived needs

Always only trying
Outcomes occur by accident or fate
Reality sets in
When breath is all I need

      In the air

Walking to The Actor's Play

Spiritual intersection
within my heart
Watching breath expel
Loneliness

The *Hunger Games* are real
In The Tenderloin
They call the very poor
Working class

Tell me sunshine
Your whole planet perforated
Working girls climb night skies
Burning from the hip

I invisibly move through street corners
Men gather radio singing
familiar blues, I glimmer faintly
Young man calls to me, "Yo! Momma!"

Mixed Messages

She ran across busy street into dark night
With Instructions for a funeral—
Lavation in Sunloy Laundry Building invites
spirits to meet without comment

Breathe in every drop
as if it makes any difference
Every soul ever lived
takes space someplace always

Aristotle's lungs took this air before Pink's
Being across oceans means nothing
save for time pulled long without end—
One moon under one sun somewhere

Strangers no longer
Eating Paella at a main square
Colombian tells of cold nights
where tortured ghosts sit steps away

Dark shadows sense
inebriated souls—
Gremlins on shoulders
calling out names, whispering faults

Echoes of laughter
color Croatian prisms in dust swirls
Hermitage at the top of the mountain
holds a wide lensed view.

I'm Not Afraid to Pray

If you call out to your God
Say Their name
The miracle is done—
Without sin we are blasted out

Capable, creative, messy
If we only knew what we were doing
Creation sourced by thought
Calling seconds into form

Carried by family
From birth of body to its decay
Surrounded
Always by images we make

Peace to beggars
Late day short dollar
Driving past meridian lepers
Always too few offerings

Sometimes you get a five
Can it be a living
A life without aim
Some addiction has to own you

Meridiem high noon
Breathe the soot
Standing holding cardboard sign
Black sharpie pitch to motorists says,

"See me, help me
Be my brethren
Our system has failed me
Which cracks have I fallen through?"

Finding yourself floored by desire
Taking satisfaction where you can
Living on someone's houseboat
Smelling like sour sweat up close

Going to dance parties strobe light
Through seventies songs—
Cocaine in the bathroom
Between partners

Please
God
Let this be
Temporary.

Silence After the Song

The smell of sawdust
Lingers after the blade sings
Scorched wood hangs inside
Treetops like a campfire
Even on this city street

Windswept

Blowing hard my head destabilizes
After I take a toke of my pipe
Wind settles down
To a whisper

God's greens float or
Bob like a bobblehead of
Baseball fame
On the dashboard of a long car—

But the wind today
Greeted us with such fervor
Our hair whipped about our faces
Just a bit of cold on bare arms

Outside on the street talking
To Violeta, brown goddess
In turquoise jewels living rent controlled
For a million years.

Planets Know the Answers

Rahu and Ketu dance—
Shadow planets relative to space time
Chandra's blue song surrenders
Moon nodes challenge life force

Shadows curve like serpents,
Slithering through mud after beastly rains
Black holes hold our best bodies
Trust, tolerance, generosity

Faithful, open-minded creatures
Looking inward to chakras root to crown
Interior universe, dauntless and creative
Spirit awakened in light—

Rahu, the head
Ketu, the body bicker endlessly
One question over and over
A riddle never solved.

Where do we go?
Withheld cherished souls
Sparkling lights stand in shadows
Beings with no bodies

Walking up Hyde
From Market to Geary
Slipping through patches of sunlight
Cool shadows filled with need follow.

Cream, Cream and More Cream

Cow milk makes us butter
A tasty deleterious spread
Cashew vegan so much better
Melts on top of peas or bread

Golden flavors collect
In heated open-air cafes
Spices caught in gust or gale
Indian, Asian, Mediterranean

Cuban or Mexican rooted fare
Global visitors
Hoping off the tour bus
For plantains, tacos, something for lunch

Rain or shine they're here to stay
Different people every day
High above pedestrian walks
Riding in the sky

Saffron and curry give us joy
Leaving sugar on the table
Optimum options abound while
Others sleep on the sidewalk

We leave leftovers at their feet
Housing out of reach
Every human needs to prosper
To varying degrees

Disparity prevails
In our city by the bay
Very rich or so damn poor
We cannot afford to look away

Under Lantern's Light

Red vest red shoes
Elderly Asian woman traverses
Under the overpass
She gives the Queen's wave

To halted motorists
Celery stalks grow long
From her shopping bag
Calms vertigo's exasperation

Faith in unicycle's perch
Pretend control
Gleeful reminder of
Youthful abilities

Holding predecessors in continuity
Her ancient homeland
Synthesizes American existence
Good luck is realized in acceptance

We are each other's society
Judging those
More or less valued
As belonging

Made up rules sanctioned in fear
Unnecessary distinctions
Determinations
Dismantled beliefs in false starts

Her children's children
Will live free of discrimination
Their own self-assurance the royal jelly
Pollinating persimmons in multiplicity

Essential Boy

Marine estuary
Low tide gazebo
Stonehenge port of Oakland
West coast rocks

Around goose families
Mother hisses loud
When we step too close—
To five soft clumsy furry babies

Small child beguiled by goose poop
Walks barefoot in black sticky sand
Dry engine oil seeped from heavy boats
Big rig caravans infuse

His soul oblivious to global crisis,
Gazes up to an elusive moon in mid-day sky
Engaged he is essential to
Humanity's best self.

Revelation

Darkness in still waters
Consciousness created within safety
Tucked away in roots
Deeply held long fixes

Vague years limiting worldly wounds
Feeling tiny regrets forging incongruity
Above the glorious Source Mind
Old memories, my so called spirit turned

Someday human
Like blustering winds that
captured temptation's dissent into time
clearing space debris

Then waking up in empty Akashic records
freedom from body or hope or despair
my literal renewal, this
hidden collaboration worthy of joy

Ripe in revelation
Flash of divinity
Guided presence completely inclusive
Waiting on welcome

Gone

Witches causeway rides a blue bridge in Vallejo
Skeletal key in hand reveals
the secret life of bones—Ta-phono-me

Talking bones embedded secret keepers
Diva's diffused divinity
settles in swirling clouds

Cooperating with authorities
Telling everything that happened
to flesh and bone since their demise

Before unearthing microscopic
nicks and scratches
breaks or fractures

Evidenced by water signatures wet and wild
Weary proof of tired bones
considered adversary

Denoting events that simulate existence
millions of years ago
Proving that nothing lasts forever
but crumbles leaving only bones

Dancers Flight

Bare but not naked
Red lips greet solemn face
Deliberate flight
In trance her delicate chin

Rests on another's arm
One shin pressed against her calf
Braced knee pushed by her thigh
Until they twist spinning velocity

Fly in tandem
Red & yellow flowers
Grow from her torso
Hover in redundant beauty

Midair leap, arms flung wide
Lavish voluntary voyagers
Delineated against harsh bright lights
Voluptuous vulnerable vigorous turned vaporous

Both dancers appear in
Mirrored walls
Audience and light crew in background
All captured in a Kodachrome click

Unruly Spectator

I found a place to be today.
Japanese baths hot soaking
mineral waters with other women,
Naked Strangers

Supple lithe bodies plunge ice cold
Exhilarated envy captures attention
Washed away fears
under skin stretched so tight

Dreams burst internally
Made real through intention
Souls rinsed clear
Egos, towel dried hang near

Just to be naked
Unadorned
In the presence of other women
I have a place to be today—

In silence we nod at each other
Lights held low
Deaf and mute in hazy fog
Unruly spectator lays back with eyes closed

III.

On Arrival

Uncapped sound frequencies not heard by humans
Cross land and sea
Before being sucked up in stone cold
Air-conditioned airport

Bones chilled dry
Dense heat swats insects just to feel a breeze
Looking for a sign in Arabic script
Malti or English that says "Exit"

Step out into Celsius low shimmer
Bus stop hut for shade made from quarries
Everything springs from limestone here
I adjust my mask

                    And wait

Cold blooded turtles scoot about
Heated double entendre
An interim of life's grace period
I catch my breath

The rock grew from a salty sea
She was named Malta
Mele meaning honey bees, they live on the island
Her ancient temples look like her people

Smooth pliable stone
Olive skinned seasoned islanders
Toil the dry parched soil
Growing prickly pears by salt flats

Lampuki pie a favorite fish dish
Sailing the tip of a gentle wave
Surrounded by crystal clear blue
I walk on water on arrival

Summer or winter we are at home here
Everyone has their part cooking or cleaning up after
We laugh and plunge into warm Mediterranean waters

Winter's charm rests in sunshine's mild breeze
Without the crowds or heat
No one goes hungry instead we overeat
Friends visits after lunch bringing sweets

Sunday is the worst when stomachs burst
Grandfather makes us laugh. He eats the most, says,
"It's best to eat now because if we get sick we won't want to."

After dishes are done
There's talk of supper's menu
Prepared Rabbit raised for food
Ancient recipes nurture our collective soul

Underground Temples 2000 Years before Stonehenge

Cave corridors home to ancient
Stone fertility Goddess
Ample breast and belly flourished bouquet
Stemmed from her dainty ankles

Neolithic underground
"Sleeping Lady Venus of Malta"
Rounded hips, thighs, calves, upper arms
Found at *Hagar Qim* temples

Thirty-five hundred BC snapshots of
The Golden Age theory of Old Europe
Matriarchal, peaceful, egalitarian cultures
Worshiped Great Goddess

Today's beaches host taut tan
Flawless beauty
Less is best
Bikini glory

I am Venus of Malta perfected
Opulence etched in cultural norms
Seduced and guided we eat accordingly
Queens of the day touched by colonialism

Conquered and ruled by prevailing winds
One thousand horses beat the ground
Flaunting power to take humanity down
To their own demise

Walking the tight wire
Rulings from times gone by
In this brave new world
Where men continue to take dominion

Dance of the avenging goddess
hold up the severed head of demon slain
Resting her foot on her lover
She is not tyranny

He lays before her with no fear
Life blooms around them
What does he have to lose?
Everything, but only if he threatens feminine force

Supportive men do not impede the goddess
Let us distinguish
Let us not turn against our allies today
Instead rage losses toward church and state

Maltese Migrations

My father was born Day of the Dead,
Sixth child of Maltese immigrants
lived in Bayview where Grandfather settled in
nineteen hundred.

Intent on finding his fortune, he spit and shined for
profit. Junk to Antique. After twenty years he saved
enough for his wife and four kids to cross the
Mediterranean. They had four more children in San
Francisco.

Tony, my dad, grew up to be musician, artist, green
thumbed, old-time foodie, drapery-man.

Nineteen fifties single dad when mother left—
He rehearsed after work while we three tucked in
dresser drawers made up like beds listened to his
trombone swoon from behind closed doors.

Anthony, my namesake.
We age alike with silver streaks
Our broad brow hovers the same
Over favorite Islander lunch,

Fresh fish with sliced tomato soaked in
Olive oil open faced on-hard crusty bread.
Blue skies sparkle across the bay as we drive 101
home past Candlestick from SFO by way of Malta.

The Way to Brave Things

Ghosts wait all year for this
Fooling with too many
Friday the thirteenths
To overthrow any happy birthdays

Beyond some common patch of sunlight
Past the heavy veil
Coming back from where we came
October settles in mid month

Don't look back or take it slow
The taste of summer vanished
Like all that mattered were
Recollections of sparkling bays & bayous

Arranged in degrees of fate
Leading into night rains
Hitting street light reflections
Green light red light blurred in sight

October is the best month
It's the last time you see sweater weather
Without the threat of snow
Hibernation just begging to take hold

Longing to gather around
Ancient tales revamped in caves
Stirring the pot of toil & trouble
Merging sweets in goblin's eyes

Not the beneficent ones
But electrifying glittery leaves falling
Inevitably the way to brave things
Whether I lived or not

Prayer for the Dead

Talks of vitality glue the dead to me
Spirit with or without flesh we exist in complementary
Spheres one side invisible

It seemed so important yesterday
When I prayed for loves now gone
In repose they listen to Norwegian snowbirds'

Song culled to messiah coming home
Don't bother your pretty little head such things
Find a way to come to terms

Because nothing really ever is
Anything but change
Injury creates response

Unknown unseen
Until that instant when it appears
And suddenly that response is your

Identity churning
Making you You
It is you

Then change

Good Trouble

Old white woman
Prepares for exit
Fire this existence right
Out over mountains dazzling my Self

Dismiss worldly trinkets
Precious privileged possessions
Invaluable concessions held hostage
By comfort

Flowing white robes heart energy
Amethyst collected in a day
Sunrise coffee revving stimuli
My merits layered like a crossbar at the door

Blocking essential attributes
Every false eyelash fancy footwear
Confidence I assume
Thwarts my glorious intrinsically unadorned

Old white woman
Walking sunlit afternoon
Meeting you eye to eye
The world holds nothing that I want

Save for the seed of limitlessness
Worthy of worship
Our thoughts and aspirations finite
Surrounded by infinite consciousness

Old white woman come back to the streets
Rally for reversed inequities
Affecting change with more than
loving kindness.

Dreams Didactic

The great forgetting will soon end.
The mystical name of the letter I
Vidya Avidya
Sanskrit for spiritual knowledge and the lack thereof

My brain a soggy organ
Cousin to my vagina
Lubricated folds
Myelin sheath
Fatty insulators
Protectors and repairers of nerve endings

Creation's tools
From human beings to
Entire worlds
Angry naked woman
Eyes wide flailing arms
A force for good

Scares evil away
Dispersed dispelled
To galaxies afar
Full moons appear
Complete and round
Whole lacking nothing

Exquisitely reflected in
Humanity's pervasive consciousness
Lift the veil
The great forgetting will soon end
The mystical name of the letter I
Vidya Avidya.

Ocean Beach

White foam
Carries world's oceans
To shore
Traffic matches roar

Seventy years old
reading eight books at once
I cannot die yet
Breathe salt air muffled

Summer solstice energy
Expanding like heat raising
To top floor remember when
We were young

Time had no end
Now it's different
Every morning every night
Every minute

Days tumble over themselves
Imaginary lines
Meridians in tapestry
Every grain of sand holds my life

Winter solstice looms
Lunar vibes press
Inward
Conversation is such an effort

Jim Carrey Said, "I Require Color!"

Holding tight to all forty Crayola colors
Vengeance unleashed
Wild, arrogant, complimentary
Correlated big brush strokes

Almost like walking through walls
Pigmentation thick and gooey
Cave drawings, revival scenes
Recording eye to hand clues

Of strength, courage, capability
Color came later
Lapis lazuli from Afghanistan
Iranian Egyptian skies

Red ochre prickly pear juice
from Mexico
Chrome yellow turmeric
India's flavor

Arsenic green
Creates light infused foliage
Monet's French expressionism
Uses violet for atmosphere

Lustrous dull
Sunlit, shadowed
Bone black necessary
For shade

Lead white before it got banned
Then Titanium and Zinc
Monochromatic worlds reflected
Just a flick captures the light

Tweets & Chirps

Weeds of the west
Nature's balance
Sapling's bushy ends
Plants and bugs with a place to stay

"Birds are better than money
In making you happy!"
She said at the end of the night
Tweets and chirps

Joyous cacophony
Crow's competing with parrots
In flight
Truth telling creatures

Beacons of light
Sprinkled sparingly
Over the universe
Caramelized sugar baked big

Sweet song in story
Told over and over
Millions of actors
Similar tales of love and loss

Redemption tribulation
Mortification and demise
Observations placed
On an old spooky alter

Songbird Mnemonics

I swear crows know
When I step out into the day—
Caw caw caw they say to me
From the sky

I clear my throat so my retort
Rings as high as their perch "Hello Crow"
Stopping mid cacophony
Birders know the drill

One second of silence
Then cheer, cheerful charmer
Eastern blue jay sings his tale
While his west coast brother is simply Jay

Whip pour will sounds just like that
Are you awake? Me too says the owl
Seek it see bit see see see—
All the way from Nashville the Warblers howl

Purty, purty, purty Northern Cardinal shouts
Trees, trees, murmuring trees sway in the breeze
With *Zay zay zoo zee*
Warbler's black throat doing double time

Chicki tuki tiki tuck
Summer's seen better days
When *plink plink bobolink* planted
Evidence pinned on everyone

Poor Sam Peabody
Sparrows turn to kiss,
Parrots sing or chant in rhyme—
All people pleasing creatures most of the time.

Seeing a Dragonfly Is Good Luck

Muted shades shift at horizon's crest
I see it reflected in dragonfly's hover
Her delicate iridescent wingspan
Flanked against an iron grate

Looking in the window
She whispers, "Old age is rebirth"
Expansive flowering
Of heart and mind

Ever changing perspective
Maturity our best reward
Echoed by dragonfly, her final phase
Offering wisdom reinforced in perpetuity

She comes to say,
"Live your best life
Savor every moment to its fullest."
By the time I see a dragonfly,

Her youth a nymph just below water's edge
Morphed to her glorious form
Earthbound for just a minute
Before she glitters the night sky.

After lifetimes of molted struggles
Shaped by sightings and dreams
Giving confidence to what's unseen
Forgiveness an illusion as corrector

To fear, attack, defense and condemnation
Each a fancy fallacy
Responding to confusion—
Dragonfly an ancient insect

Brings strength and joy to some,
Seen as sinister by others,
A wide spectrum reflecting
Endurance, destruction, and new beginnings.

Opinions

Three-part harmony
My voice a tool
Moving and melting
Coordinating complexities

As we talk of national affairs
I speak of things we can all agree
Until a car bomb explodes across the street
Screaming dissonant tones into the fold

I cross the road for stories untold
On how I ended up here
An operatic convulsion
Battling dialogues in defense

Leaning into my perceptions
Assuming what I see is true
Dried leaves collect on the surface
I swim with death

Floating on my back
In convergent salt waters
Singing the body electric
Walt's tribute to flesh and spirit

I join the atmospheric melody
Surrounded by chaos
Reaching for crescendo
I give an empathetic ear

To pro-life people
Standing beyond the choir
Deep in their own conviction
That their truth trumps my own.

Obstreperous

Inspired by Octavia Butler's novel Parable of the Sower

Wild tumultuous
Piercing screams
Rowdy unruly freeway excursions
Piles and puddles of people—

Blood splattered past
Wanderers who continue
Onward from Los Angeles to
Rural redwoods

Cacophony flees from
Open throat rituals—
Breath out our spirit animal as we
Walk the center line on foot

At midnight we are quiet
Listening to dark skies
Where evil waits to
Attack or be attacked—

Defenselessness the best defense
Inner calm walking in
Open road riots
Pushing back against fascism

Money rules the one percent
Ninety-nine percent have voices—
Integrated exchanges
Of life force congealed

See it in our art, money, politics, sports
Films, music, poetry,
Our ecological earth care—
We will make their bones shake.

To my white bros

We all grew up
Racists
Systematic sugar coated
Racism

My heartfelt capitalistic slant
I have mine
Go get yours
Hop to it with

My foot
On your back
We presumed white
trumps black

All the while ebony pulls the shades down
Drowning out the light
Refracted illusions blasted
Interior worlds swirled about

Every planet's progression through time
Our tiny lives as creative forces
No bigger than a minute
Is all we ever are—

Strong beautiful vibrant black
Rosy pink or ensuing shades of tan
Inconsequential to life
Blood flows the same for everyone

Stop the unruly perpetration
Tell the truth
We all grew up racist
America's founders were cruel

Now we atone
Collaborate
Facilitate
Give a boost go to bat

Concede to esteem
Every kin's skin
Humans respected for merits
Deserved or not

Dismantled to the bone
Historical petty positions, another lie
Hiding systemic racism creating conditions whereby
A segment of our populace is prevented from

Building wealth for centuries
All the while defining success
Its subsequent pursuit of happiness
By money's determining factor

Will we, my white brethren choose
Diversity, equity, inclusion
Acceptance to empowerment
To keep America's promises true?

Exalted Sciences

A spiritual receiver
Science compels research of
microbes, cells, bodybuilding mavericks
Split labor multiple DNA

Found in sponge and protozoan
Makes or breaks us in familiar ways
Declare greed evil, call inclusion kind
Religion is the dope dealer

Making me feel good
For nothing
Wanting to believe
We are one with creation

Winding our way up steep streets
Moving further from the truth
Eternally grateful for all aspects of life
Promises of limitless power and of peace

Ride with me under branches
Shadowed by moonlight
Armed in crystals
Spoken word wands brushing a secret film

Covering the world's nonsense
Learning to see
Our bare feet four corners warmed
In wait we whisper revelations congealed

Deliverance comes from my one Self
Lessons learned in orbit
Running after horizon's smokey allure
Royal red sky's reflection found lizards

Their eyelids sewn
Poultice made of crumbs
Powder pounded from
Teeth and nails left to dry

Formed from multiple religions
beating the same drum
Being in awe of
Astronomy, biology, ecology and physics

Sciences exalted and sublime—
If it's monuments you want
Look around
Wondrous worlds behold

Oceans

One body
Mutated over time
Permeated over eons
Seeping into separations

Imagined distinctions
Made real
Icecaps flow from the Himalayas to the Nile
Amazon turned Atlantic

Further into freshwater glaciers
Currents bring salty oceans back
Giving everything that ever touched you
Transitioning

One big wet complete body
Transformative
Ether to flesh to ether again
Ancestors caught up in the Bardo

Leading from some long awaited
Beginning resembling their end
Tracking unseen habits
That fashioned character

Cause and effect running together
Simultaneous thoughts realized to perception
Not alone in experiencing the effects of our seeing[3]
Not alone in experiencing the effects of thoughts

EGO

My phantom expression of self
Reinforced by people I know and strangers too
Their faces tell me my worth

My shiny exterior
Craves approval
Wanting to be seen, an imagined glory

Showing my version of perfection
Stemming from an elixir for every occasion—
More often I fear being seen

Hiding in a muddy container
Telling myself I should be bold,
Both sides of a pretty penny

Tossed in a fountain turned
Patina a lovely shade of green forms on my surface
I'm not tarnished to the core

Misty energy fields move in unseen swirls
Atoms creating chemical elements to
Molecules and proteins

Existence lined on the ground like a chalk
drawing of a man shot down
Projecting my past trauma

Receiving my magnificence undefined
Ego and spirit encircled entwined
I breathe through humility centered on humanity

Uncertainty

Willow petals glitter
Sunlight reflects this day
Summer breeze flipping coins
heads or tails

Tree tops shimmer
At the highest spot
Above the heat—
We do not look up

A man in the street is screaming
Calling everyone he sees an asshole
Another man yells to him with no uncertainty,
"Get off meth, Bro!"

Summer ends, it's gone too soon
Autumn next in line to gather
Precious minutes shared in common
Our daily dose of life

Heart and lungs
Intrinsically joined
Blood and breath
Tied together by language

Recalling this fraction of time
When we are here together
Rotating between birth to death
Coming home to humans humanity united

Not the loneliest number
But full and whole
Present to each other
In no uncertainty

Can I get a ride?

Climb in my dear,
Invited my car
Side seat warmed and ready,
Windows rolled down—

Heated words exchanged,
Passenger door flips open
As we cruise the curb
Heavy metal hinge springs wide

I almost fall out
Warm breeze lifts my skirt
Fingers scrape the road
Hold on tight with knuckles white

Feels like perpetual motion,
Pulling back with all my might
Happy hour rush hour
Get out of my way

Chrysler's green hornet
Picking up speed on the freeway
Others made in foreign lands
Two door Mazda—four door Honda

Hatchback coined as three,
Seat belts and child locks have no say
In this Cadillac country where
Sunroof opens to the wild

Wind rumbling past rain drops,
Sloshed against the ground
Making it hard to see through the
Judgements I inflict

Limping along on tired tires
Blaming myself for all that l think I am
Wired in the diagnostics of my mind
Running on empty I stop on a dime.

Vallarta

When we were young
We painted the town
Da Vinci brush between our toes
Shimmering in night's cloak

Rain dripping down our lips
We grasp at laughter
Fold it under our tongues
Then blow it out like bubblegum

Bodies buzzing undercurrent
Lithe and strong
In and out of bars—
Where energy lingers after the crash of waves

Spirits and language in
Fierce uproar
Gravity's dawning distance
Bringing all the planets down

In alignment with
Green-blue matter
A Botox reality
Nooks and crannies filled with our lives

Vacations included
In the grand scheme sculpted
Remnants of myself cast in concrete
Waiting for the hard parts to

Merge with the good parts
Breathing like a metal man oil can in hand
His search for perfection
Found in the pucker of a warped lemon.

Courting Feathers Caught in a Whirl

I only want transparency
Soft caresses on my cheek
Plucked from
Tradition

Filled with promise
Good fortune in the plume
Scribbling of old
Scratching paper

Certain things you just don't say
Out loud like, "I love you"
To your neighbors or
Strangers

No one wants to hear
Christmas colors
Meshed in the Easter time of
Revival

Pastels gone overboard in deep
Blues brushed against
Brown & gray & white feathers, the
Flounce of it touching ground

Holding court
Singing a holy mantra
Under the covers
Where warmth settles at night

She loves me
Pluck
He loves me not
Bare birds blunder about

Dry leaves gather—
I swim with death
Feeling overwhelmed
Coming up for air

I needed all your words today
this Easter time of revival collecting sweets
In the remembering of Lord Jesus so close to
God, the space between is lost

Save the swoosh of the air born here
Where He is Risen
Whirling wheels gather in multiplicity
stopped and static

Listening loud
You're on your own
Getting over petty illusions of
Exclusion

Whirling gatherings—
Filled in with tiny white daisies
Clues dripping down in Stalagmites
Under the concrete bridge in the park

Reading the Tarot so that
We do not talk about you and I
In this season of
passion fruit's decline—

Wheels

It doesn't matter that we are
      Matriarchs vying for power
Acting out providence in pickleball plays,

I got to watch a crow and seagull glide today
      Lifted by God's invisible hand
Riding wind waves in the sky

      I stood, back turned away
white crested ocean tipping me forward
      blowing me down — waves, green like my eyes

      I still can see
Wheels of justice in every grain of sand
Where ambiguity dissolves the lines and

      Heirs clamor for
a rich uncle with no will
Turning tides to wheels of fortune

Big like a sparkling Ferris wheel in the sun
With bucket seats swinging
      bird's eye view of treetops sway

      You'd think blustering winds
would be enough to persuade the
windmill at Ocean Beach to carry me up

      Flying like in a long ago dream
after the fall wheelbarrow's single tire leads front
and center on a gravel path to my inner altar.

Love Warrior

Listen To myself when I tell me
I'm in love with me
When the world is like a crumpled poem
tossed to the floor—

Messy with desire,
Listen to my body's muscle memory
Visions dancing in my head
Inner guidance

I don't need reasons
to love myself
No singular song
Saying I'm enough

Just speak the words
Washed in gratitude
For these years,
My blip in time.

Listen and float
above beauty—
To safety in my skin
Feeling accepted by me-

Open the crown of my head
Rising up to the sky
Let drama dispel along with
what I make up in my mind—

Jack Lalanne once asked me
how it felt to be young, beautiful and rich?
What a line!
He was eighty six.

I was younger then,
beauty is subjective,
he assumed rich,
because that's when I sold real estate.

I don't who I am anymore—
Only sure that I'm a love warrior
standing in this broken world
answering the call to love.

Endnotes

1   *A Course in Miracles,* Workbook Lesson 120

2   *A Course in Miracles,* Workbook Lesson 84

3   *A Course in Miracles,* Lesson 19

About the Author

Antoinette Vella Payne was born in San Francisco, California in 1951. She was named after her father, Anthony Vella, who was an artist, musician, and drapery man. Her mother, Jean Vella suffered schizophrenia and the disease was passed on to her two brothers. This background provided for an intense and colorful experience growing up in the San Francisco Bay Area. Raised by her stepmother, Therese Vella from the age of 5, along with her two brothers and her half-sister, Antoinette was 22 before she met her biological mother. She started writing poetry in her early twenties on the backs of scratch paper as she worked for the telephone company as a cord operator. Lacking any encouragement, she put down the pen for more than forty years. During those years, gathering life experiences, Antoinette was able to come into the truth of herself. In her mid-sixties, after a full career as a realtor and raising her daughter as a single mom, she picked up the pen again. She is currently living her dream as a semi-retired realtor and full-time poet and friend to poets. She writes daily, reads at open mics and hosts a monthly hybrid open mic reading series on 1428 Haight Street, San Francisco.